Come On In

This course has been produced as part of the Bible Reading Fellowship's celebration of the Bible in their 75th Anniversary year. It is dedicated with thanks to all those who have encouraged Bible reading in their church as an integral and valuable part of the Christian journey.

COME
ON IN

A practical guide to
understanding the Bible

DAVID WINTER
AND ANNE FAULKNER

 The Bible Reading Fellowship
OPENING THE BIBLE

Text copyright © 1997 David Winter and Anne Faulkner

The authors assert the moral right to be
identified as the authors of this work.

Published by
The Bible Reading Fellowship
Peter's Way, Sandy Lane West
Oxford OX4 5HG
ISBN 0 7459 3525 7
Albatross Books Pty Ltd
PO Box 320, Sutherland
NSW 2232, Australia
ISBN 0 7324 1567 5

First edition 1997
10 9 8 7 6 5 4 3 2 1 0

Acknowledgments
Unless otherwise stated, scripture quotations are
taken from the Good News Bible, published by The
Bible Societies/HarperCollins Publishers Ltd., UK,
© American Bible Society, 1966, 1971, 1976, 1992

Scripture quotations with the reference (NRSV) are
taken from the New Revised Standard Version of the
Bible copyright © 1989 by the Division of Christian
Education of the National Council of the Churches of
Christ in the USA.

A catalogue record for this book is
available from the British Library

Printed and bound in Malta
by Interprint Limited

Contents

Foreword

In 1922 the vicar of St Matthew's Parish Church, Brixton in London hit on a scheme to encourage his congregation to read the Bible. Each week he produced a list of daily readings, and for each day a short note introducing and explaining the passage chosen. It sounds—and was—simple, but it obviously met a need. Other churches asked if they could join in the scheme, and very soon the *Bible Reading Fellowship* was formed. Now, seventy-five years later, it is one of the world's most widely used schemes of Bible reading, with its daily notes, *New Daylight* and *Guidelines* in regular use in about sixty countries, and around 100,000 daily readers in Great Britain. The *Lightning Bolts* range of Bible reading notes for 11–14 year olds and *Livewires* Bible adventures for 8–10 year olds have recently been added to the growing range of Bible reading resources.

The church in Brixton had hit on a way to meet a real need, and that need has increased over the past seventy-five years. Even among regular church-goers, survey after survey shows that today only a small proportion of people read the Bible regularly. Some say it's 'too difficult', 'obscure', remote from their everyday experience. Others are very honest about it, and say that finding time for regular Bible reading has had to take second place to other demands on their time— work, family, home, leisure activities, hobbies and so on. Some new Christians have genuinely tried to 'get into' the Bible, but failed. Its language, ideas and culture simply seem foreign to them, however hard they try.

Yet it is a commonplace of Christian belief that God 'speaks' to us through the Bible, which Christians often call 'the word of God'. It is the touchstone of the Church's doctrine. In the words of the Second Vatican Council in 1966, it teaches 'faithfully and without error those truths which God wishes us to know for our salvation'. In the words of the Thirty-nine Articles of the Church of England it 'contains everything necessary for salvation'. So how has it come about that a book so central and vital to the life of the Church and the Christian has become a foreign book to many of us?

Well, it's no use simply bemoaning the fact! If people—even committed Christians—don't read the Bible there has to be a better explanation than that they can't be bothered, and there has to be an answer to the problem. We hope that this course book, and the group studies that it is intended to support, will be part, at least, of the answer. All *Come on in* asks of its participants is that they do just that—*participate*. We've tried to assume nothing, except a willingness on their part to give up a few hours of time, hopefully in pleasant company, to think about the Bible and its message.

We've tried to start at the beginning, as it were, so some people may find some of the material a bit basic and even obvious. Please bear with us! Because for others, new to the Christian faith, or without a long background of Sunday school and church, it's those vital basics that are often the missing link to understanding.

Come on in is designed for use in groups—quite small groups, preferably of six to ten people. But where it's not possible to get a group together, a person working on their own, will, we hope, also find the material stimulating and helpful. Although it *looks* like a book, it's really a *course*, which means that it asks you not just to read it but to *do* it. It assumes that you are willing to be an active participant in the process of discovering what the Bible is, how it came into being, and what it can mean in your life.

We should be delighted to hear from people who use this material, so that BRF can continue to provide the resources which best serve to bring the message of the Bible alive for you. Our hope is that, seventy-five years after the BRF first came into being, we can do our part in a very different kind of world to make the Bible a familiar and friendly book for thousands of people.

David Winter

FOREWORD

About this course

Session material and timings

All the material you will need is included in the text for each session, which lasts about one hour and thirty minutes, without time for coffee. You can, of course lengthen or shorten that time to suit your needs, and you may not want or need to use all the material provided. For example, if discussion works well, you may not choose to use both Bible study questions in the session. Equally, some of the activities may not seem appropriate for your group—please feel free to pick and mix!

For each session you will need...

As far as possible, every person taking part in the sessions should have a copy of this book. This is not only so that everyone can follow the chapters, but also so that by completing the various worksheets, participants will have a record of their learning at the end of the course.

If you are a group leader you will need to look carefully at the session in advance of the meeting so that you can gather the necessary equipment. You will need to provide paper, pens or pencils, and photocopied jigsaw pieces for all sessions. For some you will need to photocopy other sheets, for example, the prism in Session Five and the pie charts in Session Six. You will need glue for Session Five.

Worksheets

The worksheets are all identified by a small jigsaw shape in the top corner. As the course progresses you can use these to record your thoughts or insights and any questions or ideas that occur to you as you work with the material. The worksheets may be photocopied if you so wish.

Versions of the Bible

There are many versions of the Bible available today, and members of the group may have different translations. You may decide to all work from the same version, or you might find a mixture of translations helpful, as they can add to the understanding of the texts. The choice is yours. A selection of the versions available would be:

Good News Bible

A version of the Bible that uses basic or simple English, using a principle known as 'dynamic equivalence'. This means that at times it is nearer a paraphrase than a strict translation—but it also means that it is much easier to read for modern people than other versions. This is the version we have used in preparing this book.

New International Version
A modern translation widely used in churches today. While keeping the 'speech rhythms' of the King James Version, it uses good modern English. A reliable translation based on up to date knowledge of the Bible texts.

New Revised Standard Version
The most recent revision, this is an updating of the Revised Standard Version, which achieved wide use forty years ago. It sets out to avoid 'sexist' language. It is regarded as a highly accurate translation, based on modern textual knowledge.

Revised English Bible
A revision of the New English Bible, which was published in the 1960s. This is a translation which makes no attempt to reproduce the language or rhythms of the King James Bible, but to approach the Hebrew and Greek texts in a fresh way.

New Jerusalem Bible
This is the latest translation from Roman Catholic sources, based on the original texts and using good, standard English. Unlike all the other translations, it uses the Hebrew word 'Yahweh' for the sacred Name of God in the Old Testament.

It is worth saying that all translations are simply that—attempts to convey to the reader the words and ideas originally written in Hebrew and Greek. Differences between them largely arise from the difficulty of conveying the precise meaning of ideas expressed many centuries ago and recorded in manuscripts which are themselves copies of the original manuscripts. But all the translations listed here are conscientious attempts to arrive at the truth of the scriptures as originally given, and the modern reader has no reason to doubt their reliability and authenticity.

Jigsaw pieces
The idea of making a big, unfinished jigsaw runs all through this course. For each session you will need photocopies of the jigsaw piece opposite. Cut them out, and, if you choose to, mount them on thin card. The text makes it clear how these are to be used; you will always need one piece each and in some sessions you will need several pieces each. It is suggested that each time jigsaw pieces are completed they are put on the floor in the middle of the group, or on a central coffee table. The jigsaw pieces can be used in the closing reflections of each session.

Reading aloud
When reading the introductory material for each session, and when looking at the Bible passages we suggest that these are read aloud in the group, which would be best done by one person. Do remember that not everyone wants to read to others—ask people to volunteer, rather than expecting them to do it.

Bible materials

For Session Six you will need as many examples of Bible reading notes as you can find. Ask your minister what is available in your church and send for the BRF material on the form provided on page 63 of this book.

Closing reflections and prayer

Each session ends with a short period of reflection and prayer. The format for these is the same all through the course. You may find these suggestions helpful if you lead this part of a session.

- Put a lighted candle or an open Bible (or some other focus) in the middle of the group before this part starts.

- Keep a pause at the end of the Bible Study discussion to settle people down.

- Take your time over any writing or use of jigsaw pieces; this should never be hurried.

- Try to have enough space for people to be able to move a little, and to have space in the centre of the group.

The Collect

The Collect for Bible Sunday (Advent 2 in the Alternative Service Book) is used each week, but with a different emphasis. Read it together, then pause before reading the prayer based on the phrase in bold. Pause again for you all to pray your own prayers, either in silence or aloud.

The Lord's Prayer

A different version of the Lord's Prayer is given for each session. This will give you a chance to use some unfamiliar words to a very familiar prayer. You may want to read this slowly together.

The Grace

The different Graces suggested for the end of the time of reflection and prayer also attempt to widen experience and to include the less familiar. The Grace in Session One is taken from the ASB and those in subsequent sessions are all Celtic prayers taken from *The Celtic Vision* edited by Esther de Waal and published by Darton, Longman and Todd.

Anne Faulkner

Hints for those who lead groups

If you find yourself leading a group through this material and you are not very experienced at this, these tips may help you:

- The room needs to be big enough for everyone to be comfortable, but not so big that the group is lost (church buildings are not always ideal).

- Make sure that everyone can see the other group members.

- Everyone should be able to hear. We are not always sensitive to those who are hard of hearing, but it should not be left to them to ask for assistance.

- Think about how easy it is to hear each other in the room: beware of noisy traffic outside, noisy people inside!

- It should be possible to ventilate the room and to heat it as necessary.

- If the group is to meet in your house, who will answer the phone or the door? Who will attend to the children? The dog? Other domestic demands? The group should not be interrupted once it has started, except by any latecomers to the session.

- Make sure that you have all that is needed for the session before it starts: copies of sheets, pieces of jigsaw photocopied for each member of the group etc.

- Supply pens and paper where needed. People do not always remember to bring things to meetings even if the individual group members have been asked to do so—if they forget, your foresight might save someone from feeling awkward or left out.

- Your job is not to be the expert who knows it all, but the encourager who listens, the one who asks a few well-chosen questions, the one who stimulates discussion and is generally aware of the shy or the overconfident. Sometimes you may need to be a diplomat, and politely tell someone to be quiet.

- Encourage everyone to speak one at a time; sub-conversations are not helpful, unless you have planned it that way.

- Do not feel that every moment needs to be filled with speech. Groups are often afraid of silence, but it can be helpful to pause to think for a moment before you all move on.

• Tea or coffee can be served at the start or at the end of each session.

• Make sure everyone knows how long the session is expected to last, and keep to the agreed timings. It can be irritating if a session starts late, and very inconvenient if it goes on past the stated finishing time.

Hints for those who lead groups

SESSION 1
A bird's eye view

Introductory material

The Bible is not really 'a' book, but a library of books. The first, and largest section, the 'Old Testament', consists of the Hebrew scriptures. That's to say, it's the 'Bible' that Jesus would have known as a Jew of the first century. The second, and smaller section is the 'New Testament', which tells the story of the life, death and teaching of Jesus, describes the birth and growth of the early Christian Church and includes a number of 'letters' written by the apostles to some of those early churches.

There is no one 'author' of the Bible, though the traditional Christian view is that its true Author is the Holy Spirit. As the Creed says, 'He spoke through the prophets'. The same idea is found in 2 Peter 1:21 (NRSV): 'No prophecy ever came by human will, but men and women moved by the Holy Spirit spoke from God'. The second letter to Timothy puts it even more strongly: 'All scripture is inspired by God'—the Greek word is *theopneustos*, which means 'God-breathed'.

However, there is no suggestion that the people who actually wrote the Old and New Testament books were acting as scribes on behalf of the Holy Spirit, simply taking down his words from dictation, as it were. Clearly they were individual people with their own ideas, interests and agendas. But the difference between what they wrote and what others wrote which is not considered to be scripture is that element of direct inspiration from God. It's not without reason that the Church calls the Bible 'the Word of God'.

The period covered by the writing of the Bible is unclear, but is probably well over a thousand years, from the earliest elements in the Old Testament to the last book of the New. Most of the Old Testament was originally written in Hebrew—the only exception is possibly some of the books written during the exile. By the time of Jesus there was alongside the Hebrew scriptures, which were read in the synagogue week by week, and often learnt by heart, a Greek translation of the scriptures, known as the Septuagint. It would seem that the New Testament writers were familiar with this version.

The New Testament, of course, was written in Greek, which was the common language of the Mediterranean world. Jesus spoke in Aramaic, a Hebrew dialect, and a few words of that language are to be found in the New Testament, usually echoing a particular phrase or expression that Jesus used. The most obvious example is *Abba*, 'father'.

Until the discovery of the Dead Sea Scrolls in the late 1940s, biblical scholars had no manuscripts of the Bible older than the early medieval period. Obviously these were copies of copies. But the Dead Sea Scrolls offered a veritable treasure chest of ancient biblical manuscripts, with the text of every book of the Hebrew scriptures except Esther. These were, of course, much older, and hence much nearer to the original. Consequently modern translations of the Bible often incorporate improvements to the text drawn from the Scrolls—usually a footnote draws attention to them.

However, the biggest surprise was to find how *few* differences were to be found between the Dead Sea texts and the ones we had been relying on. The accuracy of those copied texts is a tribute to the dedication, reverence and skill of the copyists. This is further evidence that what we have in our hands, in a 'common or garden' modern Bible, is very, very close indeed to the original text of the scriptures. God not only guided the writers, but down the centuries has also protected the text! This is an important point for people who fear that what we have now is a very corrupted version of the original. It's doubtful if any book older than, say, the works of Milton (seventeenth century) is based on as impressive a body of manuscript evidence as the Bible.

GROUP WORKSHEET 1

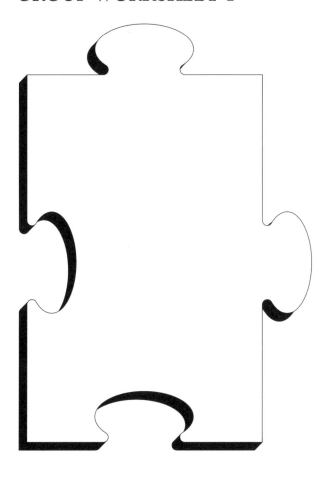

Introduction

Invite the group members to introduce themselves to the rest of the group and to give one reason why they have come, or to say one thing that they would like to get out of the course. Ask each person to write that thing on a jigsaw piece and put it on the floor in the middle of the group (or on a table)

Looking at the Bible contents

Find the contents page of your Bible and run your eye down the lists of books. In pairs or threes talk together about which ones you are most familiar with and which ones you are least familiar with. It does not matter if most of them are unfamiliar. Then, as a group, draw your discussions together. What strikes you about the contents of the Old Testament? The contents of the New Testament?

Charting the history of the Bible

Look at the two diagrams charting the history of the Bible on the following pages. What do you notice about the sequence of events? What surprises you about the history of the Bible; in the Old Testament, the New Testament or both? Use the Bible maps to put the history and the geography of the Bible together. What strikes you about the way the two come together?

Charting the history of the Old Testament

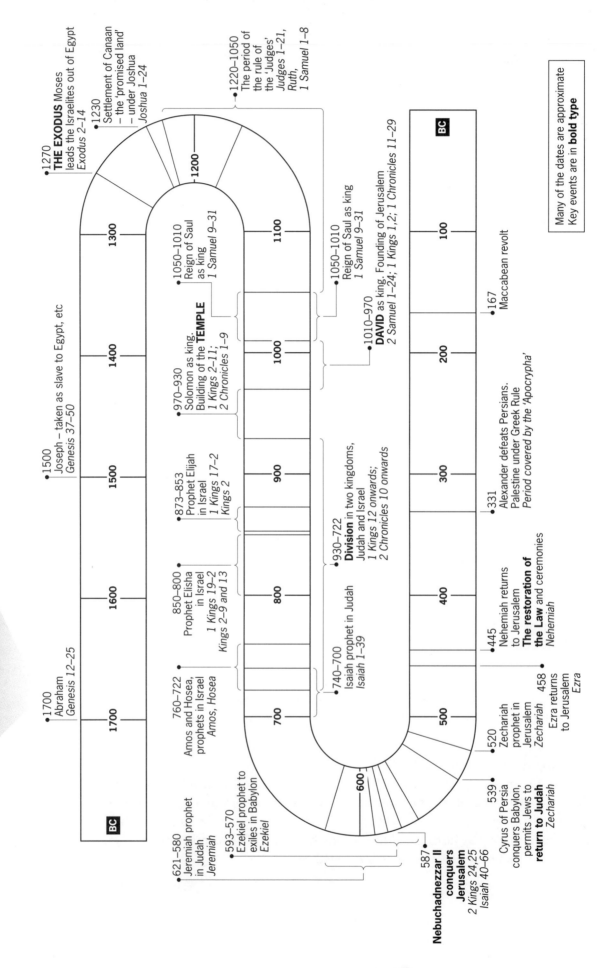

Lands of the Old Testament

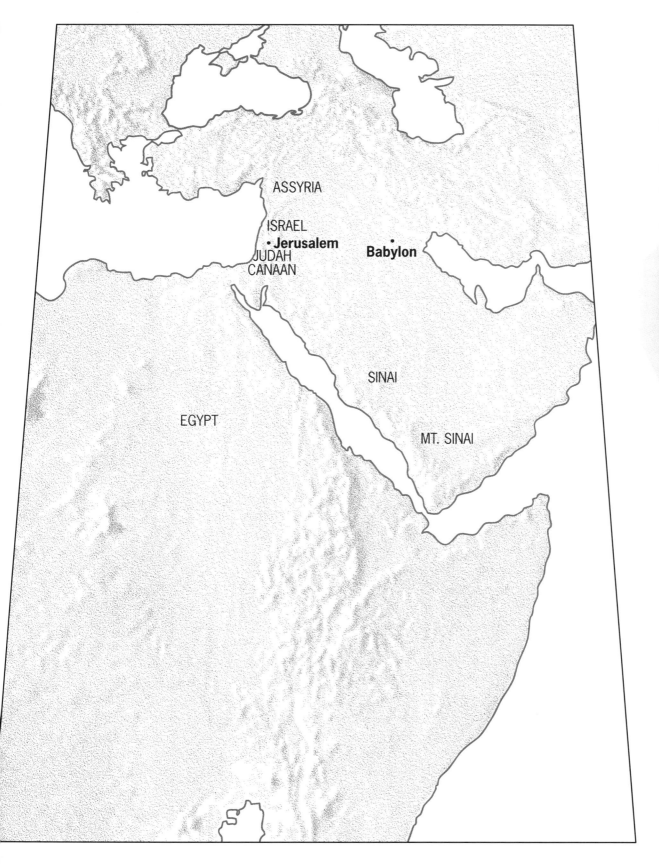

ASSYRIA

ISRAEL
•**Jerusalem**
JUDAH
CANAAN

Babylon

EGYPT

SINAI

MT. SINAI

SESSION 1: A bird's eye view

Charting the history of the New Testament

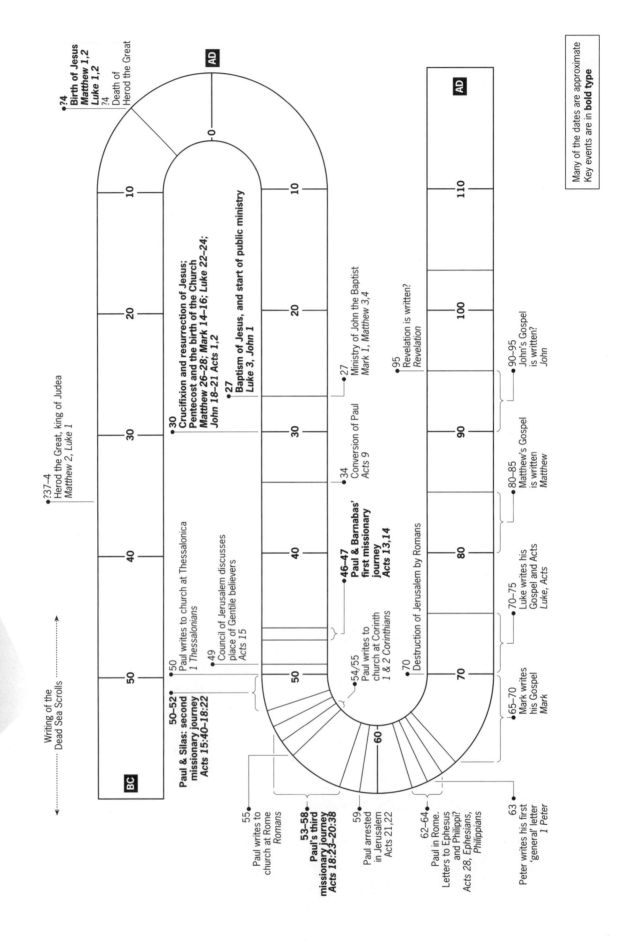

Writing of the
Dead Sea Scrolls

BC

?37–4
Herod the Great, king of Judea
Matthew 2, Luke 1

?4
Birth of Jesus
Matthew 1,2
Luke 1,2
?4
Death of
Herod the Great

AD

50–52
Paul & Silas: second
missionary journey
Acts 15:40–18:22

50
Paul writes to church at Thessalonica
1 Thessalonians

49
Council of Jerusalem discusses
place of Gentile believers
Acts 15

46–47
Paul & Barnabas'
first missionary
journey
Acts 13,14

54/55
Paul writes to
church at Corinth
1 & 2 Corinthians

70
Destruction of Jerusalem by Romans

30
Crucifixion and resurrection of Jesus;
Pentecost and the birth of the Church
Matthew 26–28; Mark 14–16; Luke 22–24;
John 18–21 Acts 1,2

27
Baptism of Jesus, and start of public ministry
Luke 3, John 1

27
Ministry of John the Baptist
Mark 1, Matthew 3,4

34
Conversion of Paul
Acts 9

95
Revelation is written?
Revelation

90–95
John's Gospel
is written?
John

80–85
Matthew's Gospel
is written
Matthew

70–75
Luke writes his
Gospel and Acts
Luke, Acts

65–70
Mark writes
his Gospel
Mark

AD

55
Paul writes to
church at Rome
Romans

53–58
Paul's third
missionary journey
Acts 18:23–20:38

59
Paul arrested
in Jerusalem
Acts 21,22

62–64
Paul in Rome.
Letters to Ephesus
and Philippi?
Acts 28, Ephesians,
Philippians

63
Peter writes his first
'general' letter
1 Peter

Many of the dates are approximate
Key events are in **bold type**

Lands of the New Testament

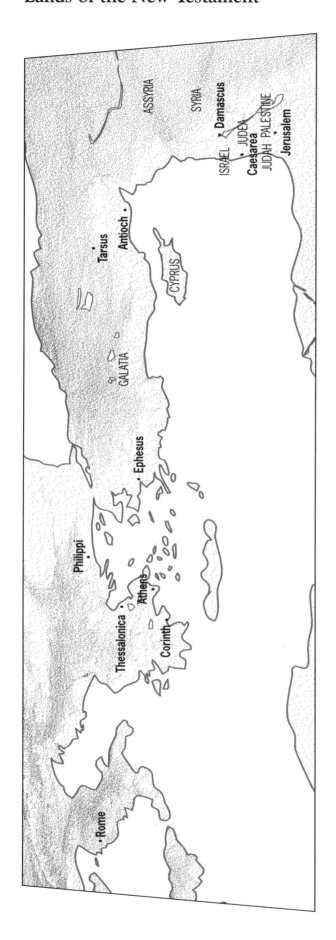

Passing the message down

Split the group into pairs, give one person from each pair pencil and paper and ask them to sit together at one side of the room. Allocate consecutive paragraphs from chapter 1, 'A bird's eye view', starting on page 15 to the remaining group (it doesn't matter if you don't have enough people for every paragraph in the chapter, but you need to allocate from the top of the chapter and continue through in consecutive order). Ask members of this group to sit opposite their partner, facing them and to read their paragraph out to their partner. Everyone is to do this at the same time and the person with the pen and paper must write down what their partner is saying to them. Set a time limit for this to be done.

Now invite the writers to read out what they have written, starting with the person who was given paragraph one and so on through the chapter.

Discuss together the following points:

• How accurately was the text recorded?

• What were the difficulties?

• What are the difficulties in passing the message of the Bible down through the generations?

• How have these difficulties been overcome? How might we continue to overcome them today?

Bible Study

Read this passage together:

2 Peter 1:16–21
The 'prophetic message' confirmed by human experience and expressed in human words as the authors were 'moved by the Holy Spirit'.

Consider these questions:

1) What evidence does the author of this book offer for the authenticity of the stories about Jesus?

2) Agree on three words which sum up the reason why the author wants the reader to take the scriptures seriously.

Reflection and prayer

Pause for a few minutes to reflect upon what you have discovered in this session.

Think of one thing that has occurred to you or one thing that you have learnt and write it on the jigsaw piece at the top of your group worksheet. This can be done in silence or you can each read out what you have written as you put it down. If there are any general insights which you all agree on, you might like to write these on a jigsaw piece and put it on the floor with the other pieces from the beginning of the session.

Collect for Bible Sunday

Blessed Lord, who caused all holy scriptures to be written for our learning: **help us so to hear them**, *to read, mark, learn, and inwardly digest them that, through patience, and the comfort of your holy word, we may embrace and hold fast the hope of everlasting life, which you have given us in our Saviour Jesus Christ.*
Amen

Take the following phrase from the Collect and use it as a focus for prayer and reflection:

Help us so to hear them: *Blessed Lord, in order to really hear what you are saying in the scriptures, we need to listen attentively to the words we read, and want to hear your word. We pray that we will not just listen for what we want to hear, but to what you want to tell us.*
Amen

The Lord's Prayer (in its traditional version)

Our Father, who art in heaven, hallowed be thy name; thy kingdom come; thy will be done; on earth as it is in heaven. Give us this day our daily bread. And forgive us our trespasses, as we forgive those who trespass against us. And lead us not into temptation; but deliver us from evil. For thine is the kingdom, the power and the glory, for ever and ever.
Amen

ASB Rite B

The Grace

The Grace of our Lord Jesus Christ, the Love of God and the fellowship of the Holy Spirit be with us now and for ever.
Amen

SESSION 2
Understanding the plot: the Hebrew scriptures

Introductory material

The Jewish scriptures—the Old Testament—consist of 39 books, and divide into five main sections. Taken as a whole, they relate the dealings of God with his 'chosen people', the Hebrews, the Jewish people, or 'Israel', over a period of considerably more than a thousand years. They tell the story of his communicating with them, describe how various men and women encountered God and understood his purpose for them, and include both poetic and prophetic insights into the nature of the 'one, true God', what the Bible calls 'the God of Abraham, Isaac and Jacob'. So far as we know, the Hebrews were the first people to think in terms of a *monotheistic* God—a God who was One, rather than many. That was their defining belief, the thing that marked them out from the nations around them. The Old Testament is the story of the gradual unfolding of the truth about that 'God who is One'.

The first five books of the Hebrew scriptures make up what is called the *Pentateuch*—the five books of Moses, as they are known. The first two, Genesis and Exodus, tell the story of creation, the 'fall' of mankind, and the early history of the Hebrew people as descendants of Abraham through to the time of their slavery in Egypt and 'exodus' under Moses. The books of Leviticus and Deuteronomy are largely concerned with the 'Law'—not just the Ten Commandments, but all the other rules and regulations which made up the Jewish religious and ethical code at the time. (The book of Numbers features the details of an early census of the people of Israel).

The next books—Joshua to 2 Chronicles—are basically 'history' books. They set out the history of the people of Israel from the settlement of Canaan to the establishment of the monarchy. Three short books—Ezra, Nehemiah and Esther—provide pictures of life during the time of exile when the people were under Babylonian rule.

The next section—Job to Song of Songs—contains the great 'wisdom' literature and poetry of Israel, and includes the Psalms, which have been part of the worship of believers for at least two and a half millennia.

The last two parts of the Old Testament are the writings of the great prophets of Israel, with the so-called 'major' prophets (Isaiah, Jeremiah and Ezekiel) first, and then the 'minor' prophets (Daniel to Malachi). Incidentally, they are not 'major' or 'minor' because of their relative importance, but simply because of the length of their writings!

The Old Testament was probably actually compiled over a period of less than a thousand years, from many sources. Jesus regarded it with great respect as expressing 'the Word of God', and so Christians, too, have revered these books and found in them priceless insights into the truth of God.

At the same time, it can't be denied that there are things in the Old Testament which Christians find strange, and even distasteful. The story of creation in Genesis, for instance, clearly comes from a pre-scientific age. This doesn't mean that it isn't 'true', more that it doesn't express truth in the way in which modern people expect to find it. Often the most profound truths can only be expressed in stories—think of the parables of Jesus. But we are a literalistic lot! Our motto is, 'Just give me the facts', even when the 'facts' would either be beyond our comprehension or less helpful than other sources of truth.

So the early chapters of Genesis may seem strange to us. But other parts of the Old Testament are not just strange, but shocking. The Lord apparently orders many massacres of Israel's enemies, and even seems to take delight in the slaughter of their women and children. At times the picture of God seems little different from that of other tribal deities of the time. Yet alongside these apparent crudities there are moving and unique reflections of God's mercy, forgiveness and (a typical Old Testament word) 'loving-kindness'.

Perhaps the clue to understanding and appreciating the Old Testament from a Christian perspective is to grasp the doctrine of *progressive revelation*. That's to say, the picture of God offered by its authors grows sharper and clearer as time goes on, and their experience of him deepens. It isn't that *God* changes, more that human perceptions of him change as we learn—over the passing centuries—more and more about his dealings with us. Of course, for Christians that revelation becomes clearest of all in the person of God's Son, Jesus, whom we accept as the long-promised Messiah. In practice, this means that Christians tend to read the Old Testament through New Testament eyes, which enables us to find riches and insights in it which are not visible to others.

Mind you, that also can raise the problem that we are failing to read the Old Testament (which we could properly call 'the Hebrew scriptures') *on their own terms*. Sometimes we need to think ourselves back into the history or culture of the Old Testament if we are really going to understand what its writers were trying to say. That's especially true of books such as Isaiah, where Christian interpretation can sometimes prevent us from appreciating the message it had for those who first read or heard these words.

All of these are good reasons for seeking some help in reading and understanding the Old Testament. It was the 'Bible' that Jesus knew, loved and lived by. These were the 'scriptures' that the apostles Paul and Peter spoke of. They are not, in some ways, as accessible to us as, say, the Gospels, but they really do repay the reader who comes to them with patience, faith and an open, enquiring mind—and is prepared to accept some help! The Old Testament sets the scene for all that God wants to reveal to us of his truth. From it we can gradually discern the ways in which he is radically different from the gods of the 'heathen'. From it we can begin to see emerging his great, over-riding purpose—to draw to himself a 'people for his own possession'.

GROUP WORKSHEET 2

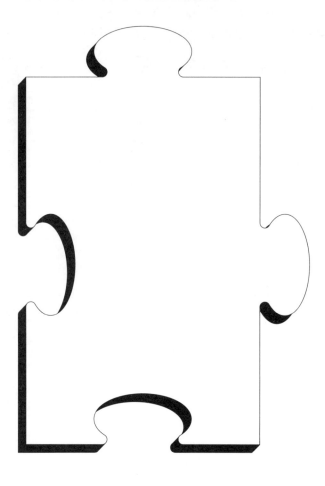

Introduction

Invite the group members to talk about memories they might have of times when they have celebrated something special. It might be an annual event which had particular significance for them one year, or a one-off occasion which holds special memories. When you have spent some time talking together, ask each person to complete the sentence:

My favourite celebration of the year is...

because...

This doesn't necessarily have to be a religious celebration, it could be an anniversary, a birthday or a special occasion which your family might celebrate together.

Looking at the Old Testament

Look again at the Old Testament contents page of your Bible and discuss how the books fit into the bookshelf diagram opposite. On a piece of jigsaw write the names of three books of the Old Testament that you know most about. On a different piece of jigsaw write the names of three books that you know least about. Put the jigsaw pieces on the floor (or table) in the middle of the group and

Books of the Old Testament

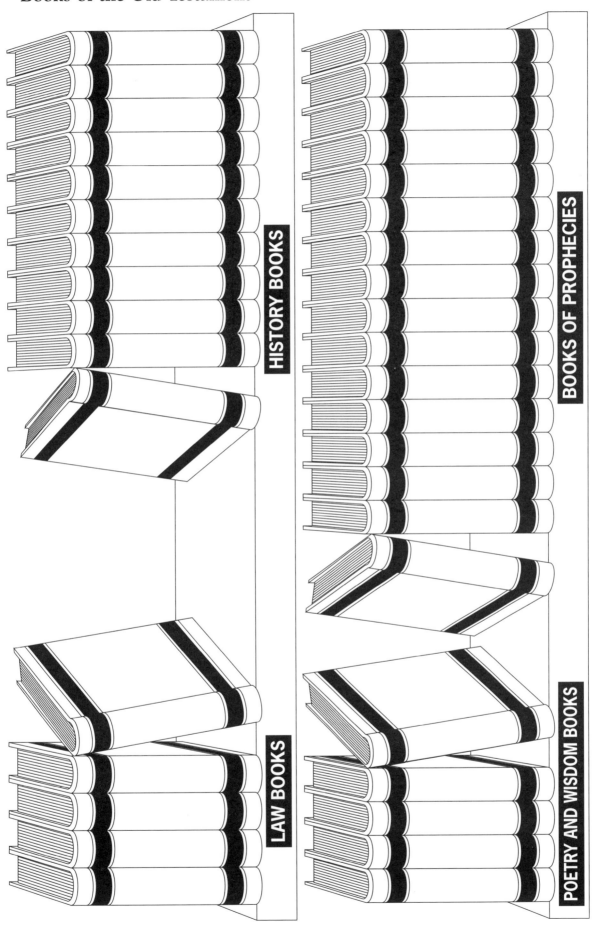

HISTORY BOOKS

BOOKS OF PROPHECIES

LAW BOOKS

POETRY AND WISDOM BOOKS

SESSION 2: Understanding the plot: the Hebrew scriptures

27

arrange them so that the lists of the books you know best are together and the lists of books you know least are together. Compare the two lists. Are there books that everyone is familiar with? Are there books which no one knows much about?

Imagining an Old Testament celebration

Read this summary of the Passover story and then talk about how much of the story group members already know. Where have you heard about the story? What do you make of it?

The Passover

Many years after the death of Joseph, the Jewish people were slaves in Egypt for over two hundred years. They thought that God had abandoned them for ever, but he called Moses to help them escape to freedom. Moses consulted Pharaoh on many occasions, but Pharaoh would not let the Jewish people leave. There followed a series of disasters that struck the Egyptians in the form of plagues: water into blood, frogs, gnats, flies, death of the animals, boils, hail, locusts and darkness. But still the people were not released. Moses gave instructions to the Jewish people about the final awful disaster which would strike the Egyptians. The angel of death would pass over the land of Egypt and kill the firstborn son in every Egyptian household. The Jews were given detailed instructions about how to prepare for this event. They were to kill a lamb, dip a sprig of hyssop in the blood and mark the outside doorposts and the lintels of their doors with the blood; the angel of death would then know that theirs was not an Egyptian house. The lamb was to be roasted (not boiled or eaten raw), and eaten with bitter herbs and unleavened bread, (yeast in bread takes time to rise, and they were to have very little warning when the time came to leave). They were to eat quickly, dressed in their travelling clothes, with their sandals on their feet; they were to stay indoors until told to move.

The Jewish people did as they were told and at last they were free to take all their belongings and leave Egypt, as the Egyptians mourned the death of their firstborn sons. At first the people were elated at being free, but when they reached the shores of the Red Sea they came to a halt and started to grumble. The Egyptians, realizing that their cheap labour had gone, gave chase to the Jews in their chariots. Moses held up his hand in faith, the waters of the Red Sea parted and the Jews all walked to the other side—to freedom. The pursuing Egyptian armies were drowned as the waters returned to cover them. God had heard the cries of his people and they were free at last.

FROM EXODUS 12:1–13

The Passover meal

Make a list of the ingredients of the Passover meal mentioned in the story, then write each ingredient on a piece of jigsaw and put these pieces on the floor with the others. The Jewish people still celebrate the Passover today, not only in order to remember that their ancestors were brought out of Egypt, but also to remember their own individual deliverance.

Look at the diagram of a seder dish, which is always on the table when the Passover is celebrated in families. Some of these symbolic foods are mentioned in the story from the book of Exodus that you have just read; some have been added over the centuries to give the festival a deeper significance for those who keep it:

- The shankbone of lamb: to remind them of the Passover lamb

- The *haroseth*, a mixture of chopped nuts, honey, apple, cinnamon and wine, the good things of life made up into a sticky substance: to remind them of the mortar from which they had to make bricks when they were slaves in Egypt

- A roasted egg: to remind them of God's presence day and night; also of new hope and new life

- Bitter herbs: to remind them of the bitterness of their slavery

- Carpas: to remind them of the fresh gifts and crops of the earth

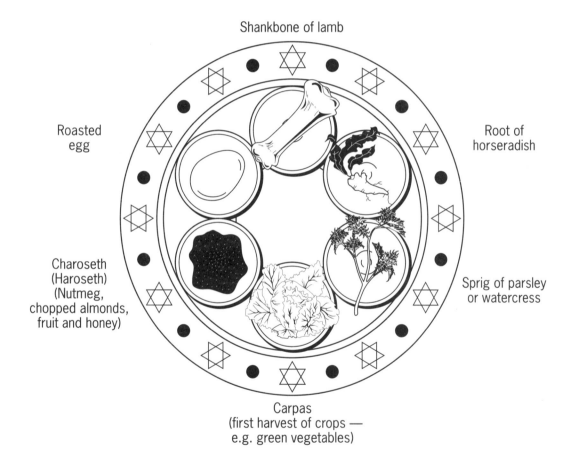

Shankbone of lamb

Roasted egg

Root of horseradish

Charoseth (Haroseth) (Nutmeg, chopped almonds, fruit and honey)

Sprig of parsley or watercress

Carpas (first harvest of crops — e.g. green vegetables)

Also on the Passover table, there would be the *Haggadah*, the book of the Passover ceremonies and the story of the exodus out of Egypt, the unleavened bread, and a bowl of salt water to remind them of the tears that were shed in Egypt.

The story of the Passover gave the Jewish people a sense of oneness as a special chosen nation. They had been saved by the angel of death, they were set free from slavery in Egypt. They crossed over the Red Sea, and so came through the water, which in the Old Testament represents chaos and disorder. They came into a new understanding of new life through God's deliverance of them, the Jewish nation, God's chosen people.

Ever since the time of these events, Jewish people have gathered every year, wherever they are, to celebrate and to remember. This remembering is not a nostalgic type of remembering, but an active, reliving, re-presenting type, that makes an event of the past become an event in the present.

As a nation, the Jewish people believed that God was with them, and that together—they and God—had gone through good times and bad. The following Bible passage echoes this:

Bible Study
Read this passage together:

Psalm 119:102–112
The scriptures as our teacher, guide, inspiration and rule.

Consider these questions:
1. If we follow the example of the speaker of these words how should we respond to the Bible?

2. What do you think it means when it says the 'word' is a lamp and a light? What difference does this make to us?

Think about the celebration which you identified as your favourite and the reason why this is so. What special things do you do to help you remember this event and why? Would it make a difference to your life if you weren't able to celebrate in this way? Why? Why do you think the Passover meal is so special for the Jewish people? Would it make a difference if they weren't allowed to celebrate this festival? Why?

Reflection and prayer
Pause for a few minutes to reflect upon what you have discovered in this session.

Remember the favourite celebration that you identified at the start of the session.

In silence thank God for that celebration and all it means to you.

In silence thank God for something new learnt about the Old Testament in this session.

Write that insight on the jigsaw piece at the top of your group worksheet. This can be done in silence or you can each read out what you have written as you put it down. If there are any general insights which you all agree on, you might like to write these on a jigsaw piece and put it on the floor with the other pieces from the beginning of the session.

Collect for Bible Sunday

Blessed Lord, who caused all holy Scriptures to be written for our learning: help us so to hear them, **to read, mark***, learn, and inwardly digest them that, through patience, and the comfort of your holy word, we may embrace and hold fast the hope of everlasting life, which you have given us in our Saviour Jesus Christ.*
Amen

To read, and mark*: Father God, not only do we need to hear your word, and to listen hard, we need to read it for ourselves, to read it silently and out loud, and to pause to notice what it says. We pray that we will allow our lives to be changed by what we read.*
Amen.

The Lord's Prayer

Our Father in heaven, hallowed be your name, your kingdom come, your will be done, on earth as in heaven. Give us today our daily bread. forgive our sins as we forgive those who sin against us. Lead us not into temptation but deliver us from evil. For the kingdom, the power and the glory are yours now and for ever.
Amen

ASB RITE A

The Grace

The grace of God be with you,
The grace of Christ be with you,
The grace of Spirit be with you,
And with your family,
for an hour, for ever, for eternity.
Amen

SESSION 3
Getting into the
New Testament

Introductory material

The New Testament centres around the person and authority of Jesus Christ. The Gospels set out to record the deep impression his life, teaching, death and resurrection made on the first disciples. Three of them—Matthew, Mark and Luke—are very similar, with many passages almost word-for-word identical, suggesting that the writers are using a common 'source' of material. They are known as the 'synoptic' (it's Greek for 'one-eyed'!) Gospels. The Fourth Gospel, John, is very different, both in style and content, though the 'story' it tells is the same one—of a teacher and miracle-worker who came to be recognized by his followers as the Messiah, was crucified and rose from the dead. John gives a more reflective, perhaps 'impressionistic' picture of Jesus—possibly the recollection of a close friend looking back on those astonishing events from a much later vantage point.

The Gospels are, in a sense, 'biographies' of Jesus, but not in the manner of modern biography. The writers are setting out to convince their readers (or hearers—most of them couldn't read) that Jesus is the promised Messiah, the Son of God, and that he rose from the dead. So they are not neutral or dispassionate about him. That doesn't mean that they were manipulating the evidence— indeed, they show every sign of being people who cared deeply about the truth— but they are organizing the material to make a point rather than to entertain or inform. Consequently, we shouldn't worry that events in the life of Jesus are presented in a different sequence in some Gospels compared to others, or that different authors emphasize different elements of the story, or of the ministry or character of Jesus. Indeed, those very differences can be very helpful in drawing out different facets of the truth about him. There wouldn't be much point in having four absolutely identical portraits of Jesus, would there?

It's generally thought that the four Gospels originated in different regions of the early Church. The earliest, Mark, has been associated with the church in Rome, and various internal clues suggest that Peter the apostle was at least one of the sources on which its author drew. It's also clear that Mark had another source of stories and sayings of Jesus, perhaps a document now lost, or equally probably the 'oral tradition' of the early churches—whole chunks of narrative, teaching and sayings which were learnt by heart and transmitted to the next generation. It's probable that the Gospels were written because of a fear that when the apostles were all dead, and in a time of intense persecution, that precious oral record might be lost, or distorted.

Matthew's Gospel probably originated in the church in Jerusalem. That, at least, is the evidence of early tradition—that it incorporates 'sayings' of Jesus, parables and sermons, which were preserved in the church there. Certainly it is the most 'Jewish' Gospel, which would make sense if it originated in the very heart of Judaism. It's most distinctive saying is, 'This happened to fulfil the prophecy...'—as an introduction to yet another quotation from the Old Testament.

Luke's Gospel, written by Paul's friend and companion, the 'beloved physician' Luke, probably emanated from the church at Ephesus, a great centre in the early days. Luke was a Gentile, and more of a 'scholar' than the other evangelists, so his book is more formal, and seems to be a serious attempt to set the life of Jesus in its historical context. At any rate, its 'preamble' claims that it is an attempt to record 'an orderly account of the events that have been fulfilled among us, just as they were handed on to us by those who from the beginning were eye-witnesses...' (NRSV).

John's Gospel is completely different—a fact that is obvious to anyone who reads it alongside the others. The basic story is the same, of course, but the emphasis is on the divine and heavenly nature of Christ, as the Son who came to fulfil his Father's will in obedience to an eternal plan. As someone has said, Matthew's Gospel begins with Abraham, Luke's in the temple in Jerusalem in the days of King Herod, Mark's in the desert of Judea with John the Baptist, and John's in heaven, at the beginning of creation. Where they each started tells us something, at least, about the journey on which they wish to lead us.

Acts of the Apostles

The 'Acts of the Apostles' tells the story of the early Church—its author, Luke, also wrote the third Gospel, of course. He was a companion of St Paul.

'Acts' presents few problems for the modern reader, because it 'simply' tells a story. Of course, again the writer, Luke, has a purpose beyond simply recording a piece of history. He wants his readers to know that the Church to which they belong is the one founded by the apostles, and that out of the conflicts and trials of the early days a united Church has emerged. All of this was important for the first readers of this book, who were facing an era of intense persecution, and also the appearance of various factions who were threatening to divide the Church.

The Letters

The Letters of Paul, James, Jude, Peter and John, and the anonymous 'Letter to the Hebrews', offer us an insight into the beliefs and life of the first Christian communities and show how the implications of the Gospel were worked out in their lives and worship.

The so-called 'Epistles'—the word just means 'letters', of course—are a priceless insight into the life of the early Church in the time of the apostles. What we need to remember in reading them is that they were *letters*, not theological treatises! Letters are to specific people in specific places, and often, of course, in answer to specific queries or problems. It would really help if we had the letters *from* Corinth, Ephesus, Galatia and so on as well!

In these letters there is a constant emphasis on the central truth of the

'Gospel', the saving message about Jesus. Through believing this message and being baptized, people were united to Christ—in Paul's familiar phrase, they were 'in Christ', they were members of his 'Body'. This membership superseded all other allegiances, of class, gender, race or social standing. They were 'all one in Christ Jesus'.

Revelation

Finally, 'Revelation' provides a vivid reminder that all that we have read in the Bible is to be seen in an eternal perspective. Through a series of visions given to a disciple called John who was in exile on the island of Patmos, it takes us into heaven itself, and offers glimpses of a future where evil has been finally eliminated from God's creation.

'Revelation' *is* a difficult book, of that there can be no doubt. It's couched in a genre with which modern people are unfamiliar, which is called 'apocalyptic'. The word means 'unveiling', and refers to 'hidden' things being revealed in a combination of symbol, picture, vision and code. Sometimes we simply don't have the 'code-breaker', and it's very difficult to know what the inner meaning of a passage is. But generally we can at least absorb the texture and passion and imagery, and being to *feel*, even if we can't fully understand, the truth which the writer was trying to convey.

For most of us, that's probably the best way to approach a book such as 'Revelation'. Let it wash over you! Don't try to unpick every vision, but rather like a modern science-fantasy, immerse yourself in the experience of the images and ideas. Of course, there is a central theme, and that undoubtedly is that although things may look hopeless now ('Revelation' comes from a time of imminent and evil persecution of the Church by the Roman emperors), God is still on the throne of the universe, evil will be finally punished and exterminated, and peace, joy and the presence of God await the faithful disciples.

GROUP WORKSHEET 3

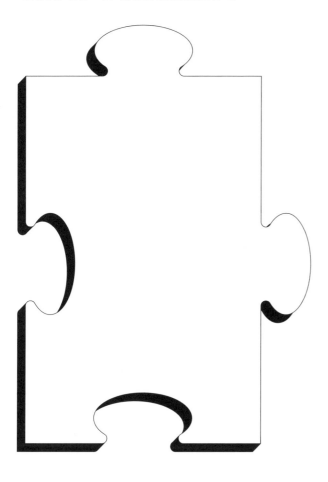

Introduction

Talk together about Easter: What do you like about it? What matters to you about Easter (it can be anything at all, not just things about church). Go round the group inviting each member to contribute to the discussion.

Looking at the New Testament

Using the New Testament contents page of your Bible, discuss how the books fit into the bookshelf diagram over the page. On a piece of jigsaw write the names of three books of the New Testament that you know most about; on a different piece of jigsaw write the names of three books that you know least about. Put the jigsaw pieces on the floor (or table) in the middle of the group. Cluster them together, as in the last session. Compare them and talk about the choices you have made.

New Testament books

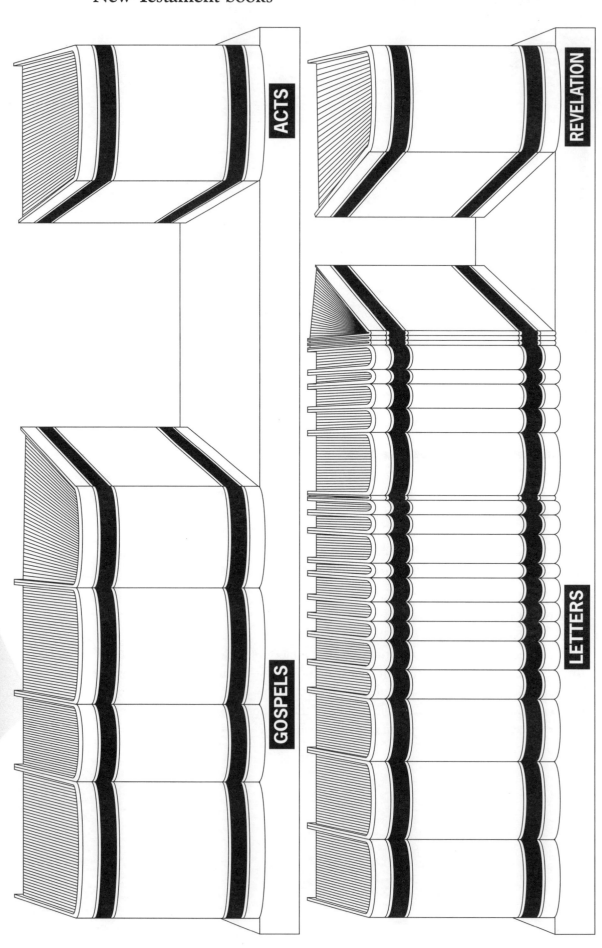

ACTS

REVELATION

GOSPELS

LETTERS

Working with the New Testament
1. Talk together about any New Testament stories you have heard of—share what you know and what you don't know. List the stories which you think are in the Gospels on the book illustrations, under the appropriate book.

2. A few stories appear in all the four Gospels (for example, the death and resurrection of Jesus, and the feeding of 5,000), some appear in two or three of the Gospels, while others are only recorded in one.
   One story that is given prominence is the Last Supper. Read together Mark 14:16–26 and then discuss some of these questions:

• At this Passover meal which ingredients did Jesus use that came from the first Jewish Passover you looked at in Session 2?

• Why did he use them?

• What would be the significance of his actions to his Jewish disciples?

   This last supper happened the night before Jesus was crucified, and has become something very special to Christians. It is the Passover of the New Israel, that is the Christian Church. You might also know it as Holy Communion, the Mass, the Eucharist or the Lord's Supper. At the last supper, Jesus told us to 'do this' in remembrance of him. That remembering is not just the recalling of an ancient custom—a nostalgic remembering—but the same active re-presenting, re-living act that we heard about in connection with the first Passover. In every Eucharist, every Holy Communion, Christians celebrate Jesus being present, as he was at the last supper on the night before he was crucified.

• What do you think it means to be the New Israel?

Bible Study
Read these passages together

John 14:25–26; John 20:30–31
The purpose of the New Testament, and its 'core'—the teaching of Jesus.

Consider these questions:
1. What do you think the disciples thought Jesus meant when he said that the Holy spirit can 'teach you everything'?

2. How can we show others that we believe Jesus is the Son of God?

Reflection and prayer
On a piece of jigsaw write down the countries where you personally know the New Testament (as part of the Bible) to be available today. (This can be done together or individually.)
Place the jigsaw piece on the floor with the other pieces.

Collect for Bible Sunday

Blessed Lord, who caused all holy Scriptures to be written for our learning: help us so to hear them, to read, mark, **learn, and inwardly digest them** *that, through patience, and the comfort of your holy word, we may embrace and hold fast the hope of everlasting life, which you have given us in our Saviour Jesus Christ.*
Amen

To learn and inwardly digest them: *O Lord, the demands upon us get greater; the idea of inwardly digesting something means effort and time. We pray that your word will change us not only on the outside but from the inside, as we slowly reflect upon it, and 'chew it over'.*
Amen

The Lord's Prayer

Our Father in heaven: May your holy name be honoured; may your Kingdom come; may your will be done on earth as it is in heaven. Give us today the food we need. Forgive us the wrongs we have done, as we forgive the wrongs that others have done to us. Do not bring us to hard testing, but keep us safe from the Evil One.
Amen

MATTHEW: 6:9–13

The Grace

God's grace distil on you
And well may it befall you
Christ's blessing be yours
And well be you entreated
Spirit's blessing be yours
And well spend you your lives
Each day that you rise
Each night that you lie down.
Amen

SESSION 4
Getting into Bible language

Introductory material

The Bible is *not* an easy book to read! Parts of it are quite straightforward, but just when we are feeling 'at home' with it, it is liable to produce a shock! It was written by many different people over a period of more than a thousand years. They lived in cultures enormously different from ours. They started from different assumptions, and shared different common values. So it's not surprising that modern readers need some help to get the most out of it. But millions of people will confirm that it's well worth the effort!

As you will have seen already, there are a number of important 'clues' for the would-be Bible reader. It is possible to summarize them like this:

When approaching a passage of the Bible, ask yourself:

• Who said this?

• To whom was this addressed originally?

• What effect was it intended to have?

• What *style* of writing is this? (e.g. story, parable, history, poetry, prophecy, vision, wise saying, biography)

• Why has it been included in the Bible? (that is, what is its *purpose?*)

• What does it say to me, now?

• What, if anything, ought I to do about it?

Categories of writing
One of the most important things in understanding the 'language' of the Bible is to appreciate the different and distinct *categories* of the various books. Not all of the Bible, for instance, is a simple narrative of 'facts'—though some of it is, of course. The problem for the modern reader is that it's not as easy to distinguish

categories of writing in these ancient documents as it is in contemporary ones.

For instance, we can generally tell when a modern writer is being ironic. We probably know when they are writing poetry rather than prose. We can recognize science fiction, fantasy books, satire and so on (though even then we sometimes get it wrong, as many writers and producers have found to their cost!).

The Bible includes elements comparable to all of those, but expressed in the cultures of a different age—so much so, that even the so-called 'experts' can't always be sure which literary category they are dealing with! To take an example, is the book of Jonah an account of something which supposedly actually happened, or is it an extended 'parable'—a story with a meaning? It's quite hard to tell from the text itself which way the writer intended us to read it, so most of us make up our minds on other grounds—whether we find the story intrinsically 'unlikely', for instance.

But on the whole it's not that difficult to decide the broad categories of the biblical writings. The Psalms are very clearly poetry, so we should not take them in a literal, prosaic way. We aren't required to believe that the sun literally travels in a chariot across the sky! The books of Chronicles and Kings are intended to be historical accounts of actual events and people—though that doesn't mean that they are necessarily infallible records of the details of those events. The 'inspiration' is in the *message*, not the historical detail.

There are some categories of writing in the Bible with which modern people are not familiar, particularly prophecy and 'apocalypse'. Prophecy is the record of those who spoke the word of God in particular situations—rebuking sin, perhaps, or holding out hope in times of distress. The typical prophetic introduction is 'Thus says the Lord...' The modern reader must resist the temptation to transfer too readily, or too literally *to ourselves and our situations now*, what was clearly spoken to a particular group of people in a particular situation at a particular time. But also we must be ready to try to discover what God is saying to us, now, through the record of that particular 'word' in that particular situation. In other words, it's not always as obvious as it might seem!

Apocalyptic literature—for example, Revelation and parts of Daniel—is the language of dreams and visions. It offers us vivid and sometimes disturbing pictures and images, which those who heard the original visions knew how to 'decode'. We may not have that knowledge! So probably the best approach is to let it wash over us, getting the 'feel' rather than worrying about the precise significance of each detail, and looking for the deeper truth about God and his purposes in history. It's not always easy, but it can be very rewarding to find in these apocalyptic writings really profound 'clues' to some of the darkest and most perplexing issues of life—suffering, for instance, or persecution, or God's ultimate purpose for the creation. Apocalyptic literature deals with issues like these, not by setting out arguments or propositions, but by drawing pictures—and many of us find that more helpful, in the long run.

So when we are confronted with a passage of scripture, it is important to start by asking ourselves what *sort* of a piece of writing is this? We may need help with that, but at least we will have guarded ourselves against the danger of jumping to wrong conclusions. After all, we know from our own experience how disastrous it can be if we fail to notice that a remark is meant to be ironic! Getting the *category* right is a very important part of understanding the whole language of the Bible.

GROUP WORKSHEET 4

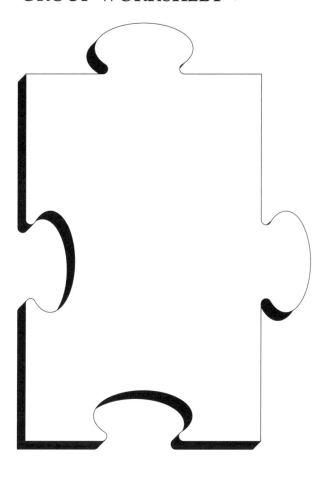

Introduction
How many languages can you speak between you? As well as those which people can speak fluently, include languages in which group members know a few words, as well as signing languages. Say some words or sentences to each other in different languages and then write or draw examples on the pieces of jigsaw.

Looking up a Bible passage
Check that everyone is comfortable with finding the book, the chapter and the verse in their own Bible and with using the index.

In pairs take one of the following references, look it up and read it.

Esther 2:1–4
Isaiah 5:1–7
Job 1:13–15
1 Kings 12:21
Psalm 100
Zechariah 8:3–5
Revelation 10:1
Proverbs 21:23–24
Mark 1:9–11

Now, in your pairs, using the Bible passage you have looked up, answer the following questions as far as you can:

• Who said this?

• In what circumstances?

• To whom was this passage originally addressed?

• What effect was it intended to have?

• What *style* of writing is this? Is it, for example:

> Story
> Parable
> History
> Law
> Poetry
> Prophecy
> Vision
> Wise saying
> Biography

• Why has it been included in the Bible—that is, what is it's *purpose*?

• What does it say to me, now?

• What, if anything, ought I to do about it?

Share what you have found out about the passages with the rest of the group.

Bible Study
Read this passage together:

Exodus 12:21–28
What it meant then, and what it might mean to us, now.

Consider these questions:
1. Christians do not celebrate the Passover now, so why do you think this story has been included in the Bible?

2. What is its meaning for us today?

On the jigsaw piece at the top of your worksheet write one thing that has occurred to you or which you have discovered for the first time during this session.

Reflection and prayer

Pause for a few minutes to think of all the different languages and of the different kinds of books and writing that you have talked about this evening. In silence thank God for the ones which have meant most to you personally.

Ask God to open your heart and mind to ask questions and find answers about the Bible.

Collect for Bible Sunday

Blessed Lord, who caused all holy Scriptures to be written for our learning: help us so to hear them, to read, mark, learn, and inwardly digest them **that, through patience, and the comfort of your holy word,** *we may embrace and hold fast the hope of everlasting life, which you have given us in our Saviour Jesus Christ.*
Amen

That through patience, and the comfort of your holy word: *Lord, we will not find it easy to study your scriptures and we will need your help. We pray that we will be given patience, perseverance and support in this task.*
Amen

The Lord's Prayer

You might like to use this version of the Lord's Prayer in French. Or, if anyone knows the Lord's Prayer in another language, you might like to use that in your prayer.

Notre Père, qui es aux cieux; que ton nom soit sanctifié; que ton règne vienne; que ta volonté soit faite sur la terre comme au ciel. Donne-nous aujourd'hui notre pain de ce jour; pardonne-nous nos offenses, comme nous pardonnons aussi à ceux qui nous ont offensés, et ne nous soumets pas à la tentation mais delivre nous du mal. Amen.

The Grace

May God make safe to keep us each step
May God make open to us each pass
May God make clear to us each road
And may he take us in the clasp of his own two hands
Amen

SESSION 5
Inspired: or inspiring

Introductory material

Modern people sometimes ask why anyone nowadays should bother to read the Bible. Isn't it, they suggest, just a collection of myths and legends, largely irrelevant to a scientific and rational age? There are two answers to those objections.

1. A God who communicates

If there is a God at all, and he is good, then surely he would wish to communicate with his human creatures, people with self-conscious awareness, 'made in his image'? The truth, in the deepest sense, of our very existence and the purpose of the creation itself are, literally, beyond us. They are, in Stephen Hawking's telling phrase, part of 'the mind of God'.

If we wish to know that truth, then we can only do so *if God chooses to reveal it to us*. If he is good, he surely wants us to know at least what is essential for us to make sense of our own existence. To leave us in the dark would be the action of a monster, not a good God. And if God is to 'let us know', then somewhere there must be a reliable record of that truth. For Christians, the Bible contains that record. As the Second Vatican Council of the Roman Catholic Church stated, 'Holy Scripture teaches, reliably, clearly and without error those truths which God wishes us to know for our salvation'. Not 'all the truth there is', you will notice, but *'what we need to know'*.

God speaks to us in many ways, of course: through nature and the created order, through our consciences, through the words of prophets and seers. All of these are valuable ways into the mind of God, but Christians believe that we have been given the clearest of all possible insights through the life of Jesus, the Son of God, who perfectly revealed God's truth and purposes.

The Bible includes all of those elements of what we call 'revelation'. It points to the order and beauty of creation, as the work of God. It recognizes and stimulates the human conscience, which is a gift of God to every human being. It records the words of prophets and seers. And it gives us a reliable and truthful record of the words and actions of Jesus.

Only by reading the Bible can we open ourselves fully to those truths 'which God wishes us to know for our salvation'.

2. The Bible 'works' in practice

All of the above would be just theory if it didn't 'work' when people actually turned to the Bible. But the evidence of Christian experience down many inspiration and guidance for daily living. The wisdom of many centuries of experience of God is distilled in the pages of the Old Testament, as they offer a slowly evolving picture of the God who made us, loves us and guides and cares for his people. And in the New Testament we have that crystal clear picture of God's love in human form, in the life of Jesus. We can hear his voice, respond to his forgiveness, be moved by his death and inspired by his resurrection. The Gospels were intended to change people's lives, and they still do!

Then we can read of the impact that the life of Jesus had on his first followers, and of the way that the Gospel message was carried all over the Roman empire, and far beyond. We can eavesdrop on the life of the early Church and learn both from its mistakes and its blessings.

The Bible is, in many ways, an inspiring book, but Christians go beyond that. They believe that it is an *inspired* book, a book that has come into being as a result of the purpose of God. Of course, the actual words were written down by fallible human beings, the people of their own age and culture. That's why at times the Bible seems elusive to us, in our own age and culture. But what they were doing was reflecting, under the guidance of the Holy Spirit, on God's dealings with them, and consequently their words can convey to us truth about God, the world and ourselves—a truth which is often matched in our own experience. It's amazing how often what we read in the Bible, written perhaps 3,000 years ago, 'rings bells' with our own need and our own experience of life and of God.

J.B. Phillips was one of the first people to try to paraphrase the New Testament into the language of the modern era. In the preface to his 'Letters to Young Churches' he wrote this: 'Without holding fundamentalist views on "inspiration", [I was] continually struck by the living quality of the material on which I was working... Again and again the writer felt rather like an electrician re-wiring an ancient house without being able to turn the mains off.'

That's what the Bible can do for those who come to it eagerly, enthusiastically, and expecting God to speak to them. In strange and unexpected ways, often, we hear his voice through the words of the Bible, we discover afresh his purpose for us, or are guided in the details of our daily lives.

It really is a book (or rather, a library of books!) well worth reading.

SESSION 5: Inspired: or inspiring

GROUP WORKSHEET 5

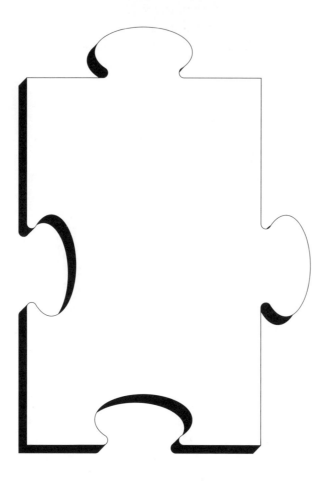

Introduction

Invite individual members of the group to choose the title of a well-known book, film or television programme, without telling the rest of the group what they are thinking of. Taking care not to force anyone to participate if they feel uncomfortable, invite group members to mime their chosen book, film or television programme to the rest of the group. They must do this without using any words—the following signs can be used to tell people whether you have chosen a book, a film or a television programme:

- Book: place hands side by side, palms up

- Film: pretend to be using a video camera

- Television: draw a square in the air

Our ways of communicating

Make a list together of all the different methods of communicating a message that you can think of. Write or draw each of them on pieces of jigsaw.

God's ways of communicating

In pairs or threes look up the Bible passages in the following list:

Psalm 119:105
Hebrews 4:12
1 Peter 1:23–25
2 Peter 1:20–21
2 Peter 3:16
2 Timothy 3:15–16
Ephesians 6:17
Isaiah 40:6–8
James 1:22–25

What does the Bible say about itself in each of these passages?

In the group share your ideas together and consider which images or pictures mean the most to you? Why?

Making a prism

Cut out the prism template over the page (photocopied onto thin card for each member of the group). On the faces of the prism write words which you feel best describe God to you. Then write the words which you feel best describe the Bible. Include words which are not in the descriptions you looked up, but which have meaning for you.

Make the prism up.

STEP 1

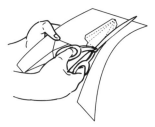

CUT AROUND THE SHAPE OUTLINED WITH A SOLID LINE

STEP 2

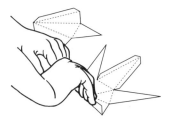

FOLD ALONG THE DOTTED LINES

STEP 3

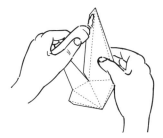

GLUE ALONG THE MARKED AREAS

STEP 4

JOIN THE TABS TO FORM A PRISM

In pairs discuss your experience of the ways in which God has communicated with you. Pool your experiences as a group and put the prisms on the floor together with the earlier jigsaw pieces.

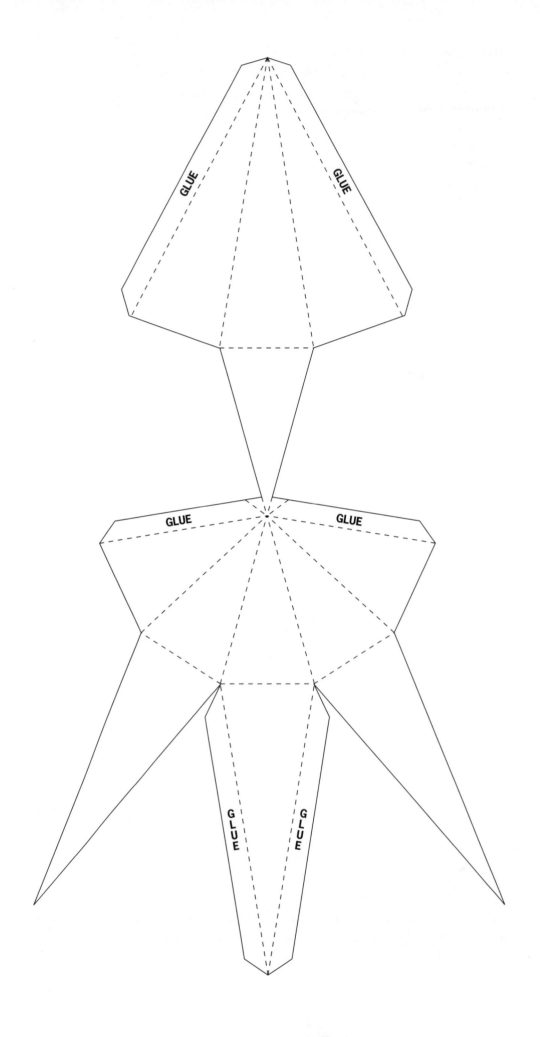

Bible Study

Read this passage together:

2 Timothy 3:14–17

Scripture is inspired by God for certain purposes and in order to produce certain results in the reader.

Consider these questions:

1. The list in this passage is restrictive. What else might you have expected to find and why?

2. In which situations in your life would you find it useful to refer to scripture?

Reflection and prayer

You may like to pick up your prism and hold it in your hands before this part begins.

Pause for a few minutes to reflect in silence on things that have occurred to you, either afresh or for the first time.

Hold your prism in your hand. Slowly read out some of the words that describe God and some of the words that describe the Bible.

In silence:

• thank God for this richness

• ask God that we may know his word well enough to be able to use it in our lives

Collect for Bible Sunday

Blessed Lord, who caused all holy Scriptures to be written for our learning: help us so to hear them, to read, mark, learn, and inwardly digest them that, through patience, and the comfort of your holy word, **we may embrace and hold fast the hope of everlasting life,** *which you have given us in our Saviour Jesus Christ.*

We may embrace and hold fast the hope of everlasting life: *Father God, the words 'embracing' and 'holding fast' convey very strong images—hugging, loving, hanging on, commitment, strength... We pray that we may be consumed with love for you, and that we may rejoice at all that you have promised us, and all that you show us in your scriptures.*
Amen

The Lord's Prayer

Our Father in heaven, holy be your Name, your kingdom come, Your will be done, on earth as in heaven. Give us today our daily bread. Forgive us our sins as we forgive those who sin against us. Do not bring us to the test but deliver us from evil. For the kingdom, the power and the glory are yours now and for ever.
Amen

CHURCH OF ENGLAND SERIES B (EXPERIMENTAL)

The Grace

May the grace of God and Jesus and the Holy Spirit
Be shielding and saving us
As Three and as One,
By our knees, by our backs, by our side
Each step of the stormy way.
Amen

SESSION 6
Getting into daily Bible reading

Introductory material

During my childhood and adolescence the Bible was a book other people talked about or read—or preached long sermons from! I don't recall ever reading it on my own, except perhaps for R.E. homework. When the Christian faith became real and personal to me, when I was a student at university, its role in my life changed dramatically. Now I found it full of wonders and delights—a book that related to the faith experience I had just had, and which addressed the questions and issues which concerned me as a Christian. I began to read it eagerly, and I suppose reading the Bible has become for me, over the length of my life, a primary means of support and strength in my own faith journey.

But I recognize that for some people, whose experience of an encounter with God is similar to mine, the Bible has not yet assumed such a central role in their Christian lives. They have tried reading it, and found it difficult or even impossible to understand. They know they ought to read it—people keep telling them that!—and consequently they feel guilty that it doesn't have the place in their lives that others expect it to have. Probably from time to time they try again, but often with the same negative result. It may be, as people say it is, the Book of God, but somehow they can't get 'into' it.

There are many possible reasons for that. After all, I came to the Bible as a student of English, with quite a literary and linguistic background. I mean, I could read and enjoy Shakespeare! So I was used to tackling problems of category, interpretation, archaic language and so on. Long words and sentences didn't put me off, and neither did apparently complicated ideas and images. They were problems that I quite enjoyed solving.

On the other hand, many highly intelligent and well-educated people today have little knowledge of ancient literature or history. They are more at home with the internet than the fishing net, so stories of outings in boats on Lake Galilee are not immediately relevant to them. They know a great deal about the modern world, which understandably occupies most of their time and thought. But they feel out of their depth in the unfamiliar world of ancient Israel or the Roman empire.

So, when they pick up the Bible, it doesn't feel or read like an 'ordinary' book, with a beginning, a middle and an end (though in that respect it's quite like some modern novels!). We can read the words fairly easily, especially in a good modern translation, but we feel we haven't understood the 'plot'.

So it's not enough simply to tell people that they 'ought' to read the Bible every day. Most Christians know that. It's finding ways to make daily reading an enjoyable, profitable and inspiring occupation that's more important.

Where do I start?

Probably not at Genesis chapter one! Most people approaching the Bible as Christians, or as Christian *seekers*, would probably find it more helpful to start with the shortest and most straightforward Gospel, Mark. My own little book *Mark for Starters* is intended for the 'new' Bible reader. It assumes no prior knowledge at all about the Bible, or Bible language. Every time a word or an idea occurs which might be unfamiliar, or even misleading, to a modern reader, there's a 'box' and a full explanation of it. Once you have got through Mark, most of the rest of the New Testament will be thoroughly accessible to you, with a little help.

That 'little help' could come from some of the books listed in my 'Basic Bible Library', but on a day to day basis it can best come from Bible reading notes, such as the ones published by the BRF (Bible Reading Fellowship). These offer the reader a section of the Bible to read for each day, accompanied by notes which both explain any problems in the text and try to point up some of the spiritual insight which it offers. The notes work at different levels. For the 'new' adult reader the appropriate notes would be *New Daylight*.

Even with such help, there will be times when you find a passage particularly difficult to understand, or, perhaps, to accept. There are 'hard sayings' in the Bible, even from the lips of Jesus—things which we may find very disturbing or which deeply challenge our present assumptions. Don't just groan and think 'here we go again!' Ask your minister, or a Christian friend, for help—and don't give up until you've got an answer. If you belong to a house group or Bible study group, raise it at the next meeting. Don't worry that this may make you look ignorant or foolish. If it bothers you, the probability is that it's bothering several others as well, even if they don't wish to admit it. Be their spokesperson!

In the early Church, as we read about it in the New Testament, the Christians were urged to help one another in this kind of way, to 'let the word of Christ dwell among them', to strengthen—yes, and even correct—each other. The Church is a family, and in a family we should be able to share things with one another and help one another with difficulties. Anyone who says that they never find any difficulties in the Bible hasn't read very much of it!

Making time for the Bible

Many people who say they would like to read the Bible regularly also say that they haven't the time to do it. Mind you, they seem to make time for three meals a day, for their favourite television 'soaps', and for the occasional game of golf or badminton!

The problem arises from the fact that at the present we don't make time for the Bible, which probably means that something else has to go, or be cut back, if we're to 'fit it in'. So, once again, it's not a matter of *time* so much as of *priorities*.

Even if we recognize that Bible reading is a priority call on a Christian's time, we still have to organize that time. It won't suddenly pop up and offer itself to us! That means looking at our daily timetable and *creating* space for it. Ten minutes a day, preferably not very late at night when concentration flags, doesn't seem a lot to ask. It could be before breakfast, or over our 'elevenses', or in the lunch hour at work, or in the evening when the children are in bed. Each of us has to work out what is best and most suitable for us. But it really does need to be fixed and regular. A pious hope that ten minutes will miraculously 'turn up' at different times each day is not likely to produce regular, committed Bible reading!

Our time of Bible reading should probably begin with a short prayer, perhaps along these lines:

Lord, you have given us your word as a light for our lives. Help me, as I read, to be open to the light of its truth, and to respond to whatever you wish to say to me through it. Amen.

After we have read, we may want to spend a few moments reflecting on what we've read. (The BRF notes often offer a simple reflection, or 'way to meditate', based on the passage from the Bible.) In that way, we remove the possibility that we may somehow think that simply reading the words will 'do us good', by some kind of magic! The Bible is definitely *not* magic, but a word from God that is to be heard and obeyed. The Letter of James puts it like this:

Do not merely listen to the word, and so deceive yourselves. Do what it says. Anyone who listens to the word but does not do what it says is like a man who looks at his face in a mirror and, after looking at himself, goes away and immediately forgets what he looks like. But the man who looks intently into the perfect law that gives freedom, and continues to do this, not forgetting what he has heard, but doing it—he will be blessed in what he does.

In other words, use the Bible as a *mirror*, in which we can see ourselves, and correct what is wrong. But we also use it as the 'perfect law that gives freedom'— the truth from God that actually sets us free! Millions of Christians down the ages will testify that the Bible has done precisely that for them.

GROUP WORKSHEET 6

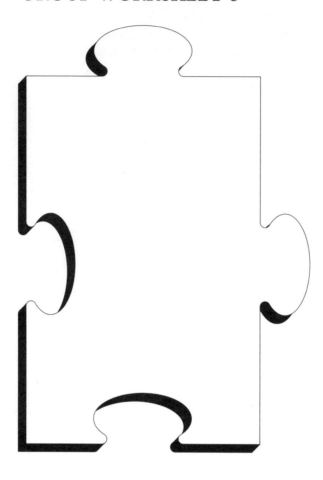

Introduction

How do we juggle with the time that we have?

Look together at the list of factors below which it has been suggested identify the nine main ways in which we use our time.

- Social

- Health

- Day to day living

- Education

- Family

- Spiritual

- Time for oneself

- Financial matters

- Sport

In pairs or threes explore the following questions:

• How do I use my time?

• What takes up the most of my time?

• What takes up the least?

Spend a few minutes discussing together and then make a personal pie chart showing a typical week. Using the nine suggested calls on your time, divide your pie chart according to the way you use your time—remember that you only have the 360 degrees of the circle to divide—no more no less!

Looking at your pie chart identify the one or two things that take up most of your time. Write them on a piece of jigsaw and put the jigsaw pieces in the middle of the group

Changing the balance

Look at your pie chart and in your pairs/threes discuss the following questions:

• To make room for Bible reading (or more Bible reading) how can the balance of my life change?

• What changes would I make to my chart?

• How would I make those changes?

Because the pie chart forms a complete circle it represents the whole of your time. If you want things to change you have to make the changes within the circle, there is no further time available. Discuss in your pairs/threes how important you think the Bible is in your life and how you could change the pattern of things to fit reading it in to your lifestyle. How could you make time to read the Bible? Or make more time to read it? What pattern of Bible reading would best suit you? Daily? What time of day? Weekly?

Now use the second pie chart to accommodate your decision.

Getting started

Discuss together the samples of daily reading resources which you have brought to the session and answer the following questions:

- What am I looking for?

- What will help me?

Decide which to use and where to get them. There is an order form at the back of this book which will enable you to order *New Daylight* from BRF if you would like to do so.

Bible Study

Read this passage together:

Psalm 119:9–18

The Word of God as something to be delighted in, meditated upon, obeyed and lived by, day by day.

Consider these questions:

1. How does this passage leave you feeling?

2. How can you act upon it?

Reflection and prayer

Spread out all the large jigsaw pieces from the six sessions, putting them flat if you have enough space, otherwise overlapping them. Notice how your jigsaw will not be complete, nor will it all fit together; our picture of God and his scriptures can never be tidy or complete.

Pause to look at and to read them (if you can).

In pairs or threes discuss what you think you have most learnt from the course. What difference, if any, will what you have learnt make to the way you think about the Bible? Pool your findings as a group.

In silence

- thank God for all that you have learnt in these sessions

- offer to him your 'new' pie chart and the decisions you have made during this session

- lay these pie charts on top of the large jigsaw.

Together slowly pray these words from the Bible Study:

Be good to me, your servant,
so that I may live and obey your teachings.
Open my eyes,
so that I may see the wonderful truths in your law.

PSALM 119:17–18

Collect for Bible Sunday

Pray the whole prayer slowly, pausing at the punctuation breaks, so that the significance of the words can flood over you.

Blessed Lord... who caused all holy Scriptures to be written for our learning... help us so to hear them... to read... mark... learn... and inwardly digest them... that, through patience... and the comfort of your holy word... we may embrace and hold fast the hope of everlasting life... which you have given us in our Saviour Jesus Christ.
Amen.

You could use this prayer at home whenever you read your Bible.

The Lord's Prayer

Our Father, May all honour you, May your rule be accepted and your purpose accomplished, as in heaven, so now on earth. Give us the food we need. Forgive us the wrong we have done as we forgive those who have wronged us. Save us from losing our faith in you, and deliver us from the power of evil.
Amen

CHURCH OF CANADA (EXPERIMENTAL)

The Grace

Be Thou a smooth way before me
be Thou a guiding star above me
be Thou a keen eye behind me
This day, this night, for ever
Amen

Appendix 1
Help with daily Bible reading

For those who would like help in getting started on regular daily Bible reading, there are a number of organizations that produce schemes, usually with explanatory notes for each day's reading. Among the best known and most widely used are:

Bible Reading Fellowship (BRF)
Peter's Way
Sandy Lane West
Oxford OX4 5HG
Telephone: 01865 748227

Daily Bible readings for children, young people and adults, and publishers of this book. Please use the form on page 63 for more information on all our resources and free samples of our Bible reading material.

Scripture Union
207–209 Queensway
Bletchley
Milton Keynes MK2 2EB
Telephone: 01908 856000

Daily Bible reading notes aimed at various age groups, from children to adults, and at different levels of comprehension.

International Bible Reading Association (IBRA)
1020 Bristol Road
Selly Oak
Birmingham B29 6LB
Telephone: 0121 472 4242

Publishers of daily Bible reading notes, ecumenical and international.

Crusade for World Revival (CWR)
Waverley Abbey House
Waverley Lane
Farnham
Surrey GU9 8EP
Telephone: 01252 783695

Publishers of *Every Day with Jesus* devotional Bible readings with a reflection on a short biblical passage for each day of the year.

Appendix 2
Building a basic Bible library

You can tell what people are interested in by the books and magazines on their shelves! So anyone who takes their Christianity seriously might be expected to possess at least a few basic books about the Bible and the Christian faith, but it's not always possible to have everything you might want or need on the shelf! The suggestions below are the ingredients for what one might call a 'Basic Bible Library' and could be put together by your church as a central pool of reference from which everyone could draw on a library borrowing system, rather than putting the onus on each individual to build their own collection.

On the other hand, many people might like to have these books in their own home, as a handy source of reference. The books would fit on to one decent sized shelf, and provide the average Bible reader with exactly the sort of instant help that they might need when faced with a particularly tricky passage of scripture.

It's a good idea to have more than one Bible version, because often comparing a passage in different translations throws important light on its meaning. A good Bible dictionary means that you can look up a word—'anointed', perhaps, or 'shepherd', or 'chronicle', or 'leper'—and find immediate information and background to its meaning in the Bible. Books of general background are also listed, which will help to explain the various parts of the Bible and put them into their historical and cultural setting.

Equally important is to have regular, daily help, and that is what the Bible Reading Fellowship, and other similar organizations, set out to supply with their daily Bible reading notes: *New Daylight*, for the average Bible reader; *Guidelines*, for the rather more 'advanced' one, *Lightning Bolts* for young people and *Livewires* for 8–10 year olds.

Translations of the Bible
Good News Bible
The New International Version
The Revised English Bible
New Jerusalem Bible
The New Revised Standard Version

Bible Dictionaries and Reference Books
The Lion Concise Bible Handbook (also available in a PC edition)
The Lion Concise Bible Encyclopedia (Lion)
The IVP New Bible Dictionary (IVP)
The Concise Bible Dictionary (IVP/Lion)
The Bible for Everyday Life (Editor: George Carey, Lion)
A concordance (e.g. *The NIV Complete Concordance*, Hodder & Stoughton)

Introduction and Background

The Book of God (Walter Wangerin, Lion)—the Bible as a novel.

The Bible as a Whole (Stephen Travis, BRF)

Ears to Hear (Studies in the Pentateuch) (Winifred Green, BRF)

Prophets and Poets (A companion to the prophetic books of the Old Testament) (Editor: Grace Emmerson, BRF)

Starting with the New Testament (Stephen Travis, Lion)

Sowers and Reapers (A companion to the four Gospels and Acts) (Editor: John Parr, BRF)

The People's Bible Commentary Series (BRF) (Devotional commentaries aimed to instruct the head and warm the heart).
    Genesis (Henry Wansbrough)
    Mark (R.T. France)
    1 Corinthians (Jerome Murphy O'Connor)
    Galatians (John Fenton)
    Revelation (Marcus Maxwell).
Please contact BRF for information of further commentaries planned for publication in this series.

Four for the Gospel Makers (Linda Foster, SCM Press)

To get you started

New Daylight (BRF)

Mark for Starters (David Winter, BRF)

Day by Day (Volumes 1, 2 and 3) A year's undated daily readings in each volume arranged in themes, with printed Bible passages, brief comments and prayers or meditations (BRF).

His Spirit is with Us: Understanding the Spirit of God in our lives (Chris Neal, BRF) Readings and meditations on the presence, role and work of the Holy Spirit throughout the Bible and in the fabric of our lives today.

Day by Day with the Psalms (Douglas Cleverley Ford, BRF)

New Daylight and Guidelines

The Bible Reading Fellowship publishes two series of regular Bible reading notes, *New Daylight* and *Guidelines*, three times a year (in January, May and September). *New Daylight* contains printed Bible passages, brief comments and prayers and is also available in a large print version. *Guidelines* contains a commentary on Bible passages, with a weekly 'Guidelines' section which seeks to apply the teaching to life in a more devotional way.

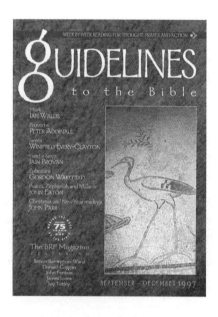

Copies of *New Daylight* and *Guidelines* may be obtained from your local Christian bookshop or by subscription direct from BRF. A free sample copy of *New Daylight* or *Guidelines* may be obtained by sending an A5 SAE with 36p stamp marked '*New Daylight*' or '*Guidelines*' to BRF.

For more information about the full range of BRF publications and about subscriptions to the notes, write to: The Bible Reading Fellowship, Peter's Way, Sandy Lane West, Oxford OX4 5HG. Tel 01865 748227 Fax 01865 773150

BRF Resources Order Form

			Price	Qty	Value
3524 9	Bible as a Whole, The	Stephen Travis	£8.99	_____	_____
2829 3	Ears to Hear	Winifred Green	£4.99	_____	_____
2599 5	Prophets and Poets	Ed. Grace Emmerson	£8.99	_____	_____
2531 6	Sowers and Reapers	Ed. John Parr	£9.99	_____	_____

The People's Bible Commentary Series

			Price	Qty	Value
2821 8	Genesis	Henry Wansbrough	£5.99	_____	_____
2824 2	Mark	R.T. France	£7.99	_____	_____
3280 0	1 Corinthians	Jerome Murphy-O'Connor	£7.99	_____	_____
3281 9	Galatians	John Fenton	£4.99	_____	_____
3297 5	Revelation	Marcus Maxwell	£7.99	_____	_____
2825 0	Mark for Starters	David Winter	£2.99	_____	_____
2598 7	Day by Day Volume 1		£10.99	_____	_____
3250 9	Day by Day Volume 3		£10.99	_____	_____
3077 8	His Spirit is with Us	Chris Neal	£5.99	_____	_____
2975 3	Day by Day with the Psalms	Douglas Cleverley Ford	£5.99	_____	_____

Total value of books: £_____

Postage and packing: £_____

Donation to BRF: £_____

Total enclosed: £_____

Postage and packing rates

Order Value	UK	Europe	Rest of World	
			Surface	Airmail
£6.00 & under	£1.25	£2.25	£2.25	£3.50
£6.01-£14.99	£3.00	£3.50	£4.50	£6.00
£15.00-£29.99	£4.00	£5.50	£7.50	£11.00
£30.00 & over	FREE	PRICE ON REQUEST		

Please complete the payment details below (all orders must be accompanied by the appropriate payment) and send your completed form to **BRF, Peter's Way, Sandy Lane West, Oxford OX4 5HG.**

Name . . . . Account Number . . . .

Address . . . .

. . . . Postcode . . . .

Method of Payment: ☐ Cheque ☐ Mastercard ☐ Visa ☐ Postal Order ☐ Switch

Credit card number ☐☐☐☐ ☐☐☐☐ ☐☐☐☐ ☐☐☐☐ Expiry Date ☐☐ ☐☐

Switch card number ☐☐☐☐☐☐☐☐☐☐☐☐☐☐☐☐☐☐ Expiry Date ☐☐ ☐☐

Issue number of Switch card ☐☐☐ Signature . . . . Date . . . .

(necessary if payment by credit card)

☐ Please send me regular information about BRF resources.

The Bible Reading Fellowship, Peter's Way, Sandy Lane West, Oxford OX4 5HG
Tel 01865 748227 Fax 01865 773150 BRF is a Registered Charity (No. 233280)
Prices and postage rates valid until 31 December 1997